# Celebrated Christmas Solos

**BOOK 2**

(UK Exam Grades 1–2)

## 7 Christmas Favorites Arranged for Late Elementary to Early Intermediate Pianists

### Robert D. Vandall

The Christmas recital is the most popular one in my wife's and my studio. We schedule three short Christmas recitals each year so that all of the students who wish to perform are included. The arrangements in *Celebrated Christmas Solos, Book 2,* are for students at the late-elementary to early-intermediate level. The carols and songs chosen are those most favored by students, as they love playing carols and songs that they know well. Short introductions and codas extend the arrangements into satisfying musical experiences. It is my hope that students will enjoy playing, teachers will enjoy teaching, and audiences will enjoy hearing these arrangements. After all, Christmas music captures the essence of the Christmas season! Merry Christmas!

*Robert D. Vandall*

## Contents

Copyright © MMVI by Alfred Music Publishing Co., Inc.
All rights reserved. Printed in USA.
ISBN 0-7390-4339-0

# Silent Night

Franz Grüber
Arr. by Robert D. Vandall

**Moderately slow and peaceful**

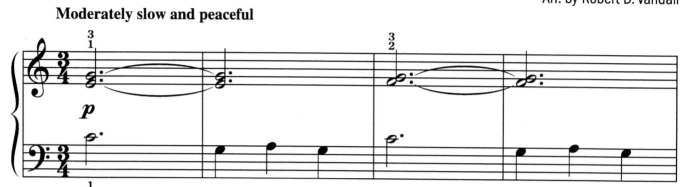

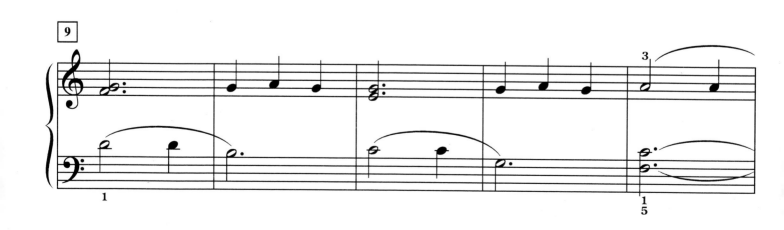

# Angels We Have Heard on High

French Carol
Arr. by Robert D. Vandall

**Fast and joyful**

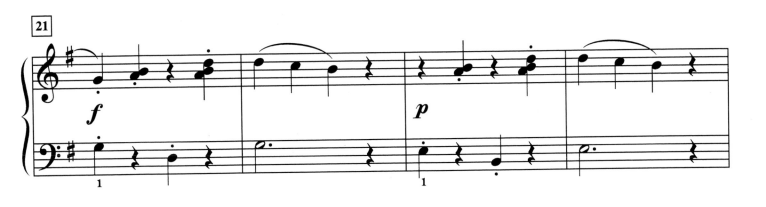

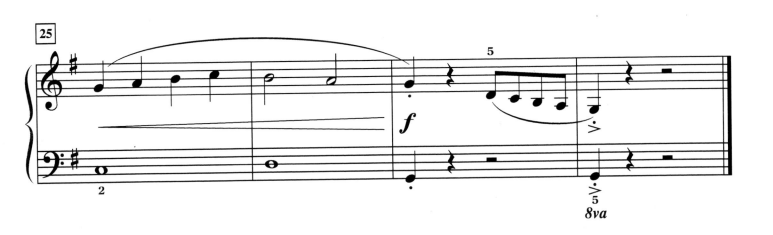

# What Child Is This?

English Carol
Arr. by Robert D. Vandall

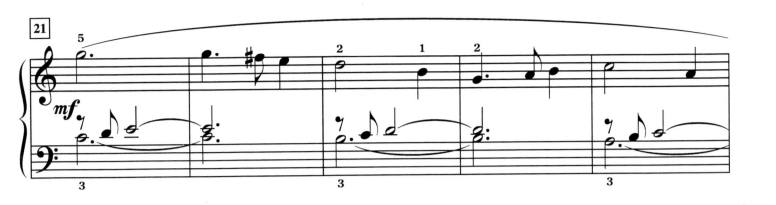

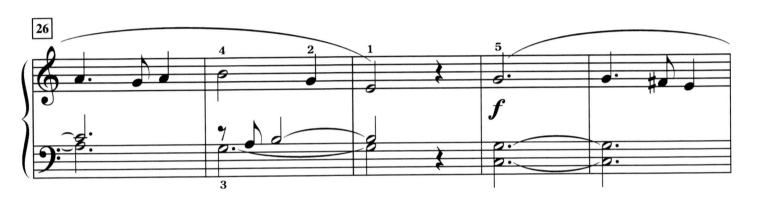

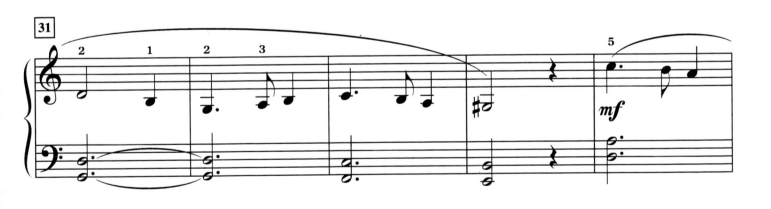

# Ding, Dong! Merrily on High

English Carol
Arr. by Robert D. Vandall

**Joyous**

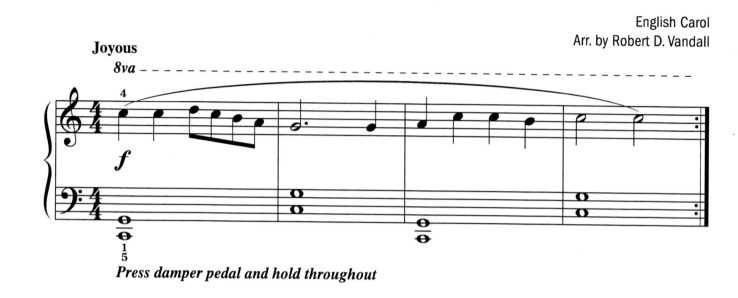

*Press damper pedal and hold throughout*

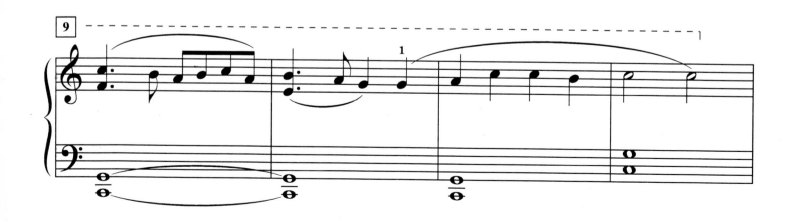

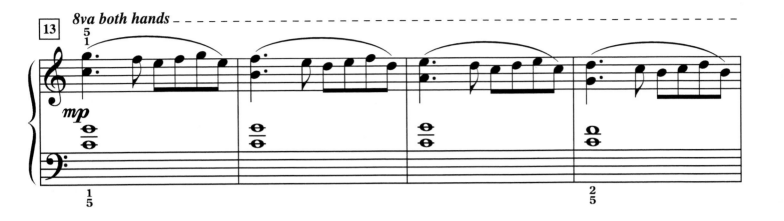

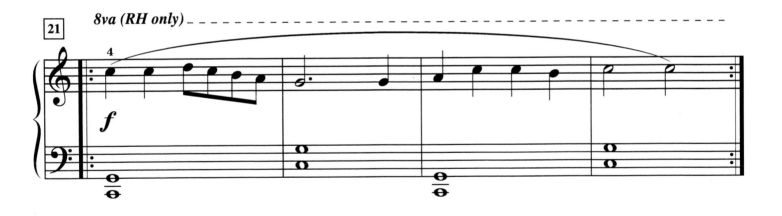

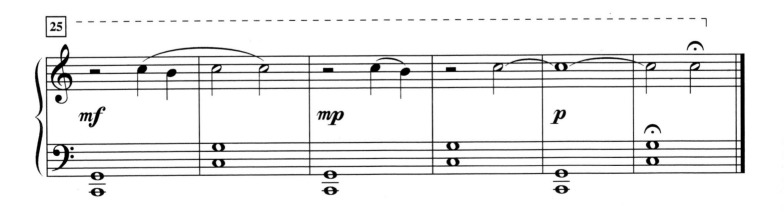

# Carol of the Bells

Leontovich
Arr. by Robert D. Vandall

**Ringing happily**

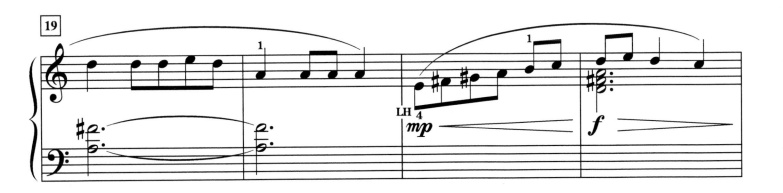

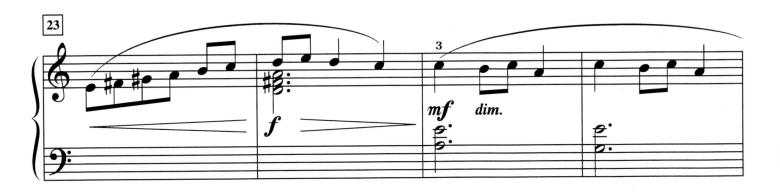

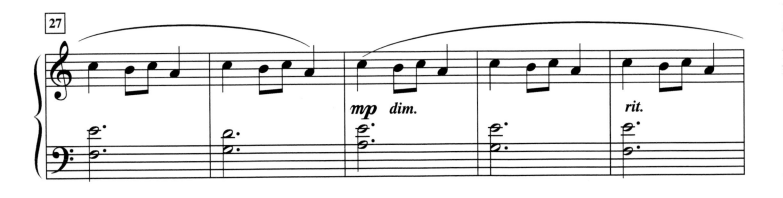

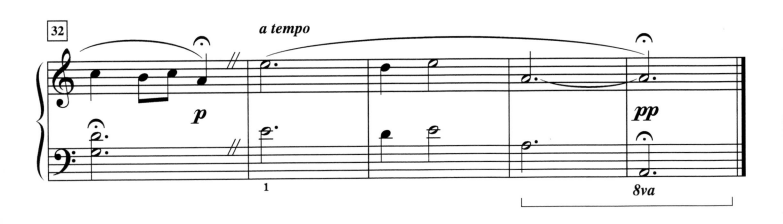

# O Christmas Tree

German Carol
Arr. by Robert D. Vandall

**Fast and dancelike**

# Frosty, the Snowman

Steve Nelson and Walter Rollins
Arr. by Robert D. Vandall

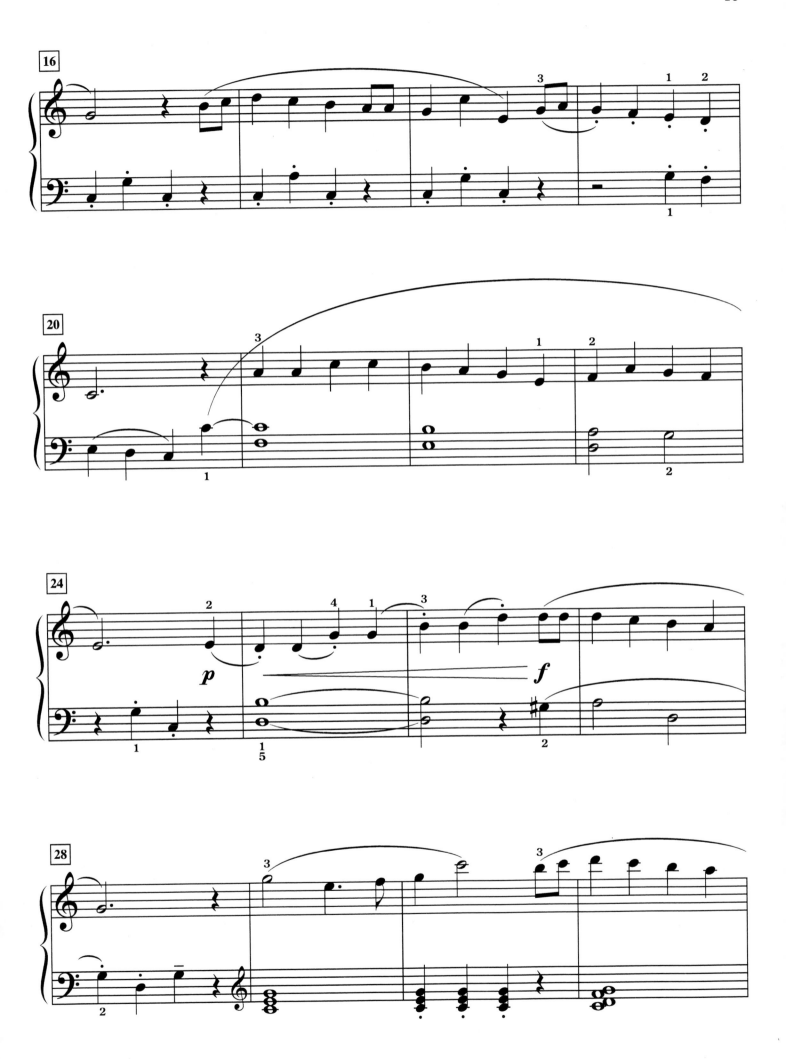

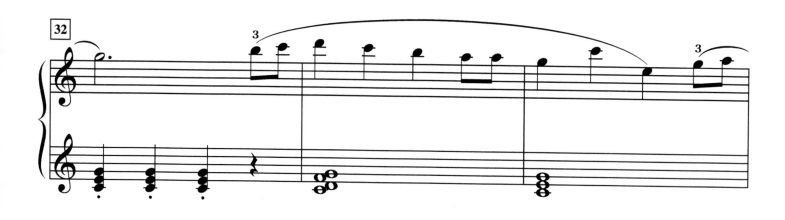

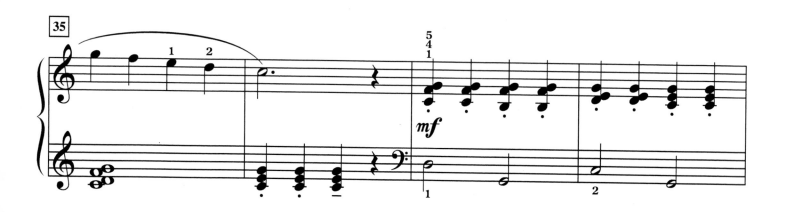

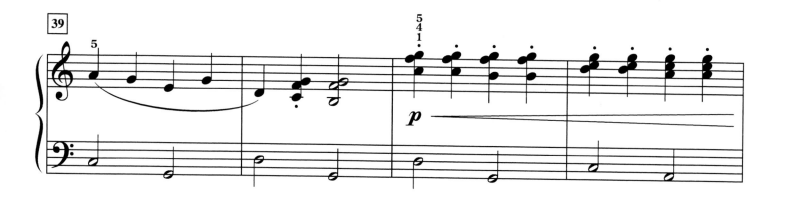

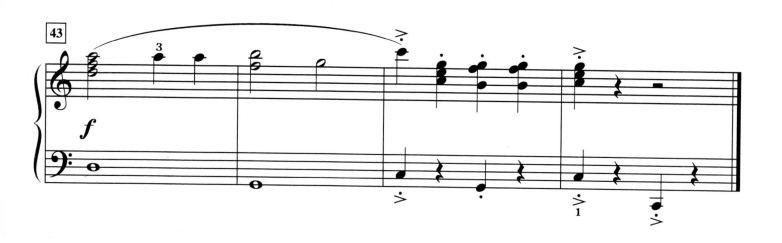